D0205948

Even So

by Gary Young

BOOKS

Even So: New and Selected Poems 2012
Pleasure 2006
No Other Life 2005
Braver Deeds 1999
Days 1997
The Dream of a Moral Life 1990
Hands 1979

ANTHOLOGIES (with Christopher Buckley)

One for the Money: The Sentence as a Poetic Form 2012
Bear Flag Republic: Prose Poems and Poetics from California 2008
The Geography of Home: California's Poetry of Place 1999

LIMITED EDITIONS

New Mexico Journal: Rio Vallecitos 2012
In the Face of It 2009
III × III (with Christopher Buckley and Derek McKown) 2007
No Harm Done 2004
The Body's Logic 2000
My Place Here Below 1996
Then It Happens 1996
My Brother's in Wyoming 1994
Wherever I Looked 1993
Nine Days: New York 1991
A Single Day 1991
The Geography of Home 1987
In the Durable World 1985
6 Prayers 1984

Even So

NEW AND SELECTED POEMS

Gary Young

WHITE PINE PRESS

White Pine Press
P.O. Box 236
Buffalo, New York 14201
www.whitepine.org

Copyright © 2012 by Gary Young

All rights reserved. This work, or portions thereof, may not be reproduced in any form without the written permission of the publisher. Publication of this book was made possible, in part, by a grant from the National Endowment for the Arts, which believes that a great nation deserves great art, and with public funds from the New York State Council on the Arts, a State Agency.

Cover illustration: *North Pasture*, drypoint by Gary Young

First Edition

ISBN 978-1-935210-33-7

Library of Congress number: 2011931997

Printed and bound in the United States of America

for Peggy, always

ACKNOWLEDGMENTS

Poems from the following previously published books appear in this volume:
Hands, 1979, Illuminati Press
    Second edition, 1981, Jazz Press
The Dream of a Moral Life, 1990, Copper Beach Press
Days, 1997, Silverfish Review Press
Braver Deeds, 1999, Gibbs Smith, Publisher
No Other Life, 2002, Creative Arts Book Company
    Second edition with an introduction by Peter Johnson, 2005, Heyday Books
Pleasure, 2006, Heyday Books

Many of the new poems printed here originally appeared in various publications:
Askew: "Fissures in the bedrock," "Last night I dreamed about a bobcat,"
    "Damselflies couple in midair."
Denver Quarterly: "A raven calls out overhead," "Sparrows glean the air."
Hubbub: "Tonight, before sleep."
Massachusetts Review: "As if the sky and the high plateaus."
The Normal School: "The earth submits."
The Packinghouse Review: "At dusk, the whine of insects," "Whenever I travel," "I am a fearful
    person," "On a still afternoon," "Shadows passed over the mesa," "Ten thousand
    years ago," "In the heat of late afternoon," "The pottery made in this pueblo."
Pulp: "I often get confused," "I have long thought of the world."
Quick Fiction: "This tumor is smaller," "The tribal guard."
Red Wheelbarrow: "Coming down the mountain," "My father has the power," "They
    had warned me about snakes."
Salt Hill: "I once found a smooth, round stone," "Shards of pottery," "Driving north
    along the coast," "When Elizabeth had died."
Sentence: "The skunks and the deer are in rut," "Near midnight, walking uphill,"
    "In western Massachusetts," "Wheeled in from the cosmos."

Many of these new poems appeared in limited editions: *In the Face of It*, C & C Press,
2009; *New Mexico Journal: Rio Vallecitos*, C & C Press, 2011; *III × III*, Warparade Press,
2007. "This tumor is smaller," "Last night I dreamed about a bobcat," "In western
Massachusetts," and "The skunks and the deer are in rut again" appeared in *The
Marin Poetry Center Anthology*. "The skunks and the deer are in rut again" appeared
in the 2008 International Poetry Calendar, Alhambra Publishing, Belgium. "Near
midnight, walking uphill" appeared in the 2010 International Poetry Calendar,
Alhambra Publishing, Belgium. "This tumor is smaller" and "Last night I dreamed
about a bobcat" appeared in *Bear Flag Republic: Prose Poems and Poetics from California*,
Greenhouse Review Press/Alcatraz Editions, 2008. "The earth submits" appeared
in *Breathe: 101 Contemporary Odes*, C & R Press, 2009. "This tumor is smaller"
appeared in *View from the Bed/View from the Bedside*, Wising Up Press, 2010. "Here in
the valley," "Two black geldings" "This morning a pair of flickers," and "I have never
experienced such a fracturing," appeared in *Cadence of Hooves: A Celebration of Horses*,
Yarroway Mountain Press, 2008. "The earth submits" appeared in *The Rose Metal Press
Field Guide to Prose Poetry*, Rose Metal Press, 2010.

My heartfelt thanks to the publishers of these books, journals and anthologies, and
to the many friends who gave their generous attention to these poems as they were
being written, in particular Christopher Buckley, Killarney Clary and Stephen Kessler.

CONTENTS

from Hands

from The Dream of a Moral Life

from Days

from Braver Deeds

from If He Had

from Pleasure

New Poems

New Mexico Journal: Rio Vallecitos

In the Face of It

from Hands

Pleine main j'ai reçu
Pleine main je donne

LE CORBUSIER

Walking Home from Work

Asphalt and gravel flex with my shoes as the heel
hits and pulls the rest of my body forward.
Ahead of me, twilight is ending
and the ragged outline of the mountain
is glazed with iridescence, each tree
singular and sure.
Each night the same. Or if not
the same, then part of one long night
that leads me to my house, there
on the high ground of the foothills.
A thin streak of gray smoke
rises from the chimney,
a string from which the house
is suspended in the darkness.
I am a block away before shadows appear
moving against the fogged
windows in the kitchen.
My wife is baking bread. A hand
reaches up and wipes away the steam.
Light spills out of the kitchen
and begins to fill the world.

First Rain

The wind plays
its tune on the bare
tangle of wisteria; a sullen
whistle that starts and stops
in short, hard breaths.
Rain streaks the window
and distorts the shrubs,
fruit trees, and dark
outlines of tools left
to rust in the field.
This weather takes the edge off
all contours. The rain erases
even itself, and leaves only
the impression of movement.
The landscape outside
is familiar, but only
in the way a jacket is familiar,
the empty skin of someone
we recognize but do not know.
I want everything
to be still, the rain
running off the porch
to stop and hang
silently above the ground,
a single star, a perfect
globe in which to read
our future.

The Doctor Rebuilds a Hand

His hand was a puppet, more wood than flesh.
He had brought the forest back with him: bark, pitch,
the dull leaves and thick hardwood that gave way
to bone and severed nerves throughout his fingers.
There was no pain. He suffered instead the terror
of a man lost in the woods, the ache of companions
as they give up the search, wait, and return home.
What creeps in the timber and low brush
crept between his fingers, following the blood spoor.
As I removed splinters from the torn skin
I discovered the landscape of bodies,
the forest's skin and flesh. I felt
the dark pressure of my own blood stiffen
against the red pulp I worked into a hand
using my own as the model. If I could abandon the vanity
of healing, I would enter the forest of wounds myself,
and be delivered, unafraid, from whatever I touched.

Secondhand Suit

In the musty racks
of the St. Vincent de Paul
I have once again fallen
in love with another man's suit.

It is not a coincidence
of style that attracts me;
this is how I will see myself,
this is what I will be.

Between the double breasts of the jacket
is a door through which
I enter the world. I feel
the blue serge, and its texture

assures me of my own texture
and substance. I have come
to this jacket, to this material,
and discovered my place here

has been justified.
The world accommodates us.
I put on the suit
and the padded shoulders fall

evenly into place.
The baggy trousers hang
with an air of contrite
overabundance.

I turn slowly before the mirror
and remember my mother once saying,
*you have the body
of a beggar, everything fits.*

Through a Stranger's House

I surround myself
with fern seed, elm bark,
and lead my way
with the dead man's thumb.
Dreams pour out of it.

I fill my bag quickly with valuables
but linger in the bedroom,
watch the glow from this thumb
filter through the damp fog of my herbs
and settle on the couple in bed.
The light seeps into them
as if they were hollow.

The Laying On of Hands

They come slowly:
women with white
crippled limbs,

holding their deformities
like frail birds.

They untie the murderer's wrists
and gently stroke a wen,
goiter or misshapen back
with a cold hand.

They bow and
return to their homes
where they are healed.

Rev. Robert A. Young (1893–1977)

> "Verily I say unto you, Whosoever
> shall not receive the kingdom of
> God as a little child, he shall
> Not enter therein."
>
> MARK 10:15

Ill, shaken and hollowed out, he remained
the best of what he had been, the mad preacher
delivering sermons to the wall, entreating
the curtains to be wary of their pride.

This man once held me
spellbound from the pulpit, the only preacher
I could ever sit still for.
If age stole his vigor and withered him,
he avenged himself with good deeds
and better. If the world was lost, spirit
was everywhere waiting to bless and be blessed.

I still see him standing in the fog
of his failed senses, hands gesturing
to a phantom couple who have come
to be married by Dr. Young, here
in the corner of the bedroom.
Do you take this woman, he asks,
do you take this man? And I hear them
answer each in turn, *I do, I do, I do.*

Winter Solstice

Birds travel toward the horizon
at a distance which makes them
indistinguishable. We know only
that they seem to be leaving the earth.
The glassy bulbs of the iris have worked their way
to the surface of the damp soil,
and the roots of the pine tree
rest on the ground like arthritic knuckles,
clumsy, useless, having given up
on everything, even themselves.
I watch the rain fall after a year of drought,
and it settles into the runoff. My yard
is a delta of tiny rivers, and the spirit,
which must be like water, flows quietly away.

Equinox

Today the light will be as the darkness; our dreams
and what we have learned to expect in their place
will be equal. The sky senses this and divides
into enormous strips of white cloud and blue.
A breeze is in from the ocean, folding the branches
and leaves of the black walnut toward the mountains.
Monarchs hang like windows of stained glass from the fruit trees.
The world cannot be more perfect than it is today,
when what we have gained is equal to all we will lose.
The sun is setting behind the eucalyptus, and already
a harvest moon rises. Tomorrow will be a shorter day.
Below me, around the table my feet dangle beneath,
alyssum and wild mint strain toward the weakening light.

The Pears

Slumped in a broken-backed oak chair,
or leaning, in the garden, against
beanpoles and smooth-handled tools,
the summer touches and slows us until
like fruit, we swell with it. My hands
have thickened and lost their grace.
I am good now only for clearing brush
or turning compost into the dull, gray soil.
What delicate work there is
the season accomplishes without me.
Scallions carpet the field around the fig trees,
and the pears ripen into yellow bells
that fall and ring into the ground
and into our arms and legs as we bend
to gather the last fruit of the year.

from The Dream of a Moral Life

O Nature, and O soul of man!
how far beyond all utterance are your linked analogies;
not the smallest atom stirs or lives on matter,
but has its cunning duplicate in mind.

HERMAN MELVILLE

Eating Wild Mushrooms

After the rain, when the earth releases
a little wheezing breath and loosens
its brittle hold on the surface of things,

wild mushrooms appear under the trees,
against logs and along the rotting
boards behind the barn. I see them lift

the ground under the quince and spread
the scallions apart and rise, and open.
I have been shown by those who know

the slick-skinned Blewit, the Prince
like a man's head, and Satyr's Beard
with its yellow mange. But for the rest

I cultivate an ignorance and pick
puffballs a particular shade of beige,
toadstools with the prettiest caps

or purple, spongy stem. What I don't know
can't hurt me. What I do know
is that mushrooms rise from the dead

to die again, to enter the death
of whatever enters the earth. When I
pick an unfamiliar mushroom and eat it

the ground gives up for once and is cheated.
It is like kissing a stranger on the mouth.
It is knowing what you are and being forgiven.

Prayer

Your attention is turned from the ineluctable
patterns in the clouds, and settles at last
on the starlings. Their fat, clumsy bodies
fail for once to disturb you. Even their chatter
you would not call music,
but it complements the light and seems
to occupy a space made for it. Secure and fixed,
you are a piece of this and for once
feel more beautiful than what you see. How could you
tolerate more? Something simple and sure falls
over the landscape and covers you.
You think you have been saved again, but you
don't know how, from what, or by whom.

Starfish

The splintered timbers of the pier
shudder and creak. A woman traces
a wrinkle in her cheek while her children
test the tension of their lines, the surge
and pull of the swells and the unseen hand
that keeps their hearts beating faster
with each sudden tug. They've arranged
rows of pink starfish at their feet.
Looking down at them is like looking up.
It is the sky we imagined
in childhood laid flat on the rough
boards of the pier. It is night,
the grease-blackened wood
tells you that, and the stars are almost alive.
Perspective is lost: the outline of the shore
is a cardboard silhouette, and there is no
distinction between the water and the sky.
The arms of the starfish
twist and curl. The children raise
the metal crabnet and pull
one last crab from the fish heads and guts.
Stars come out quickly in the sky overhead.
The night deepens and the starfish grow
darker and darker until they vanish
with the water, with the pilings of the pier,
and are replaced by our memory, our desires
and what we allow ourselves to make of them.
It is always night. There are always stars.

Under the Catalpa Trees

At first I could remove the bandages
and look at myself the way I have looked
at photographs, curious but detached.
Later I was filled with a kind of repulsion
and guilt, the same I felt
when passing cripples on the street
and I could not look away.
They tell me I'll get used to this
strange face that I cannot recognize as me,
but that is a lie. Even in my dreams
when I stand back and watch myself
chased, caught and dismembered,
it is my old face that grimaces and screams.
But it is true about the world, how it goes
on without us, or in spite of us, and even
the pain I feared would be the end of me
brings a kind of solace to these gray,
spring mornings. It does not disappoint.
I once craved latitude, the ability to become
someone different, someone strange. Now
I must learn to accept that my prayers
were answered and fulfilled. There is no good
reason for what becomes of us, but I have discovered
no malice. We move and are moved.
Standing under the catalpa trees, watching
the heart-shaped leaves open larger
than I ever thought possible, I feel comfortable
with my new face. I am even ready
for the children, for their mimicry. Let them
have my stooped walk, my grin and sullen gestures.
Then let them change.

Tornado Watch, Bloomington, Indiana

The sky, reading our thoughts
as always, blackens and grows still.
I am filled with the menace
of my own mind, of bad weather
when my chest spasms and I think
gunshot as the lightning
blinds me, and the room shatters
with the nearness of it.
The clock, the kitchen table,
the dishes swimming in their rack
pulse and glow; a purple light escapes
everything and the moment will not pass.
I cannot breathe but the air
is sweet, thick, and seems
to push its way into me.
If I could move, I would not.
Dying, suspended within us and held close,
could be like this. In my terror
or pleasure, I imagine heaven, until
from outside, a starling in the sycamore
begins his hoarse song and I go on
living in the durable world.

The Elegies

July the second, a chill wind and
unseasonable rain; another surprise
the world delights in and serves up.
Another day of mourning and of grief.

I look to the landscape, to the weather
for correspondence or prediction,
revelations from the particular,
but it is all correspondence: our pain

takes shape and holds fast to the blue
tile roofs, the glistening streets,
the endless rows of trees. We are made,
like the world, to contain our sadness, and do.

The wind moves away from shore, and a factory,
smoke rising from its twin stacks, is a
barge carrying the dead away from the city,
across the bay, endlessly. But that, too,

is a frail construction. The dead
are like angels, incorporeal and pure,
while the living belong to what is,
enter there, and inherit it all.

Seven Days of Rain

After seven days of rain the creek begins
to fall below the ferns and the crumbling
rock above the waterline. The silt
settles out slowly, and trout
rise again for flies. Steam
lifts itself from the roof and the bent
limbs of the redwood and pine. The storm
has passed and I am finally free
to work indoors without fear
of the rising waters. I unpack
boxes and trunks, arrange photographs
into a livable landscape. What can't be used
or thrown away, I release to the archeology
of closets—diplomas, letters from those
now dead, and at last, a tin box passed
down four generations to me. My mother's
mementos: a diary, brittle pressed flowers
and snapshots that could be anyone.
In a corner of the box, folded neatly
against a bag of foreign coins,
a length of heavy yellow lace still shows
the flesh-colored smudges of my mother's makeup.
Now that she is gone, this lace will
age for her, and I do not need
to lift it to my face and inhale the breath
that greeted me with each embrace
to know there is something in all of us,
anger, remorse, or love, that refuses always
to pass entirely away.

To Raise a Chimney

I climbed down to the stream and looked back
past landslide and fallen logs
to the house, and the impossible distances
where the chimney would be. Braced
against the current and the slippery bank
I lifted stone after stone
to the sound of a long, wet kiss
as the water released them.
Piled under a bay tree they sparkled and dripped,
veins of quartz glistening in the granite.
One by one I carried them up the hill.
To catch my breath I sang out loud,
hymns recalled from childhood,
as if that, too, had been a difficult labor.
Such odd strength in that cadence.
I kept its rhythm and mixed mortar
the consistency of dough. The stones
were laid down. I felt the warmth
of the mortar as it cured and set.
I climbed the scaffold, placed more stones
and the chimney rose. It rose
and the air below was drawn up and exhaled
in one unending breath. It rose and began
to moan as if the ground
had discovered a mouth to bellow through.
Looking down from that height
I had no fear of falling. I was afraid
of climbing forever, singing hymns like an angel
and moving stone by stone away from the earth.

Our Life in California

Near San Ardo the grasses tremble
and oak trees bend to the south against a constant wind.
Here our faith is tested
by the air that passes us ceaselessly
and takes each lost breath as we stumble through the hills.
The monotony of breathing, like our heartbeat,
is not the reassuring monotony
of the hills stacked row upon row
beyond our bearing and our ken.
The sun moves with the wind and will be gone,
but there is another light
coming from below, casting trees from the shadows.
There is a shadow beneath me
which moves as I move,
and the tracks I leave in the fragile grass
know more than I know of my duty here,
my worth and my chance.

At San Vicente Creek

The soul arrests at the soft, chalk cliffs
and holds there, like the pelicans leaning
into a senseless breeze thrown over
the water's stone channel.
Uninterrupted, it shifts and penetrates the fields abutting
the ocean's mean pull. The crops, docile
and dutiful, pull it closer and expand with it. This
is satisfying. There are couples
everywhere longing for this kind
of marriage; and the wind knows, and the birds
holding themselves needlessly against their own strength
know; and the soul, which measures itself against all it caresses
knows and finds a measure for the love
it embodies but cannot possess.

On Printing

Pack rats watch from their home in the eaves.
The presses are down. The hypnotic machines
rest now in their bulk like men who have gathered
for gossip or prayer. I swear I have heard them
sigh in their great satisfaction.
We are born to this work, to love set loose
upon the world; to give life to bodies, words,
the orderly repetition of ourselves. We are the tools
of increase, and multiply our common emotion: joy
at our labors, which we repeat again and again.

The Orchard in Oils

Leaves and spent limbs of the apricot
retreat in planes, one to the other
in the geography of heaven.
The sky, a shy blue, bleached and dim,
adjusts this perspective and falls away.
Color perpetuates the caliber of being.
Burning through the leaves
at the furthest reaches of the tree,
the sun leans forward, as do the apricots
propelled toward us in gold silhouette,
lustrous, ripe, the correspondence
of hunger and vision, our own desire
to repel depth, to come forward
into the rich, unfailing light.

Burning

Sometimes when the wind shifts quickly back from the woods
the flames from the slash heap surround me, and I smell myself burning.
All day a junco has watched from the fruit trees as I fed the fire.
The flames jump and the green limbs snap and hiss
but the junco stays. He doesn't know what I have done.
He leads me to the persimmon tree and begins to sing.
He looks right at me and he doesn't leave.
He must not care what's in my heart.

The Lake at Echo Park

Swallows, like the palms, were a part of the changing values
as wind twisted them to another shape and hue.
The water, too, was unpredictable. Dimpled and nervous
above the hollows, it calmed nearer to shore and reflected
a shadow beneath each tree. The lilies
and the leaves like elephant's ears held constant,
their colors unchanged by the sun which slid above the red
tile roofs of the bungalows. Water surrounded
and held us in the tiny boat, was a compass of the world
wrapped in a single broad prospect about the shore.
Old men with their bamboo poles seemed to penetrate the rounded
white walls of the temple behind them, and shared,
with the lotus blossoms, a single, shifting plane. We were shielded
by the lake, the focus of a light that insisted on distance,
so when I turned and pulled you toward me we became the relief
of depth, a full nature that seemed to allow the blackbirds
to rise from their perch on the bobbing lily pads and somehow disappear.

September Night

Clouds break before the full moon and deer step out of darkness to graze.
My shadow is lying on the still, wet grass
like a shadow in daylight. It's beautiful
to pass even briefly over the earth. How terrible
to believe in nothing. I lift my arms and the darker marks tremble.
The startled deer move in a staggered, halting line
back into the woods. The moon beats on the corrugated tin of the coops
and in this cruel and lucid light the metal roof is burning.

from Days

The world of dew
Is the world of dew,
And yet . . .
And yet . . .

ISSA

I hear and behold God in every object,
yet understand God not in the least . . .

WALT WHITMAN

She took my two hands in hers, pressed and caressed them as if she were bathing me. I held hers as mine were held, stroked her knuckles, her palms, then realized the finger I lightly traced was my own. How strange to find I could show myself such tenderness.

I don't know where the owls go when they leave this place, or if they never leave, but simply leave off calling sometimes in their hollow voices. But tonight they are here: one in a redwood beyond the creek, one high in the fir tree above the house. Rappelled through their voices, those three long vowels the darkness speaks in, I forget my own worthlessness which has troubled me all day.

My friend is dying piece by piece. His right side is paralyzed, already gone. In the time remaining, he is learning to speak again, and his good left side rages against his right. He follows each rent thought to cleavage and dead end, then backtracks and starts again. He hopes to remember, he stammers, how to draw a sentence.

I have such envy for my wife, as her belly grows, and the baby wakes, dreams and wakes again in its own new life. I wonder if she envies me, unable as she is to be outside of it, to watch as I watch, my own becoming in another.

We sat in a silence interrupted by gesture; there was nothing I could say. I rubbed his legs, and pulled the curled fingers of his hand. He tried to speak, and I think he said, I'll be seeing you. And I wondered, if that's so, how will I recognize him then.

Our son was born under a full moon. That night I walked through the orchard, and the orchard was changed as I was. There were blossoms on the fruit trees, more white blossoms on the dogwood, and the tiny clenched fists of bracken shimmered silver. My shadow fell beside the shadow of the trees like a luster on the grass, and wherever I looked there was light.

I'm reading the stars to figure my place here below. I watch the constellations slide and spill across the sky. There are star charts geared and matched to our lives, but here is the real map we are born to and fixed on. Not even the night is still. We are spinning with the stars, and heaven must wheel as well.

I last saw my mother a week after her suicide, in a dream. She was so shy; she was only there a moment. I'd called her stupid. How could you be so stupid? Eight years later she's back. What do you want, I ask her, what do you really want? I want to sing, she says. And she sings.

The baby fusses. I read a book to quiet him, and he calms. His fingers open, show a lifeline, heartline, all the fates lurking in his flesh. He's asleep when I finish, and one hand closes in a fist around my thumb. Somewhere he learned even dreams must be tethered to the earth.

Trembling and furious, the baby screams. He's tired, and his own body frightens him. I hold him by his shoulders and sing. It's a sad song, but he finally sleeps. It's a sad song, but even silence can be a terror, and a violence, and I keep singing.

The stream echoed through the canyon, and it seemed the current no longer flowed, but hovered, and was held as we were, in the insulating mist where time circled itself, uncertain of direction, until a peacock screamed, a tractor coughed, and the thousand wheels began to spin again.

The stillborn calf lies near the fence where its mother licked the damp body, then left it. All afternoon she has stood beside a large, white rock in the middle of the pasture. She nuzzles it with her heavy neck and will not be lured away. This must be her purest intelligence, to accept what she expected, something sure, intractable, the whole focus of the afternoon's pale light.

I'm a mother, too, she said, and took the child in her arms. She closed her eyes, kissed his head, smelled his neck. My baby is twenty-nine, she said, and she handed him back.

Falling limbs have taken a piece of the house each of the last two storms. I once praised this peril; it forced fear and gratitude into my life. Now I want it gone. It wakes me, and I beg, spare my wife and child, take me, like some criminal gambling with God.

Queen Anne's lace crowds the air; cicadas call from beyond the stream. Monkeyflowers rouge the hill below a pasture where six horses crop sage; and beside the road, between riprap at the river mouth, down gullies and the wasted ravines, thistles are showing us their hearts again.

In a dream that shouldn't frighten me, small birds rise and fall before my feet like leaves, like dust. It is a design of worry and regret, a pattern of coincidence and contradiction. One morning I freed a bird; later that day I killed a rat.

I walked through the camellias to calm myself, and pulled the only blossom to my face. Odd a flower so perfect, so serene, could have no scent, that my heart could be a currency for the traffic in anger.

Two girls were struck by lightning at the harbor mouth. An orange flame lifted them up and laid them down again. Their thin suits had been melted away. It's a miracle they survived. It's a miracle they were ever born at all.

A boy wandered into the woods and was lost. That night while we hunted, a neighbor dreamed she saw him in a pasture, and next morning rode away and found him there. This is the story they'll tell later; this is the story that saved the boy's life.

If we lived alone, like these clouds stalled over the valley, we could ignore the world. We'd look out on the sky; all our doors would open to the air. We could ignore the lights coming on in the windows below. We could spend each day dreaming of eternity.

Three girls discovered a man sleeping under the willows. Weeks later, the man had not moved. He'd died alone there, under the trees. When the girls returned, they each believed he was still sleeping.

Tea steeps in my old cup. Faces appear and vanish at the window. Mourning doves gather in the locust, the ginkgo, the liquidambar. What use were my travels; every moment is a journey. Do I smell ginger, or jasmine on this strange new air?

I wanted a house that could float in silence over the mountains, then a great quake tore away the earth beneath our home. A man downstream was buried alive; we can't know what he wanted. And what was he looking for at the mouth of that cave?

Boulders roll and chime beneath the current. The tiny spiked caps of the chestnuts whirr as they fall. This inadvertent music is a grace. I've whispered to the dead, and prayed in anger. When he sounds his one shrill note, even the hawk is a songbird.

My house is in ruins, but I still have a home in the hours. My friends have gone, but we are never alone. There are murmurs in the wind, a voice in the stream. A mockingbird calls from the sycamore; I can hear him. When I speak, someone listens.

Our cat was killed in the first hour of the new year. Later that night it snowed. I saw this as a sign. I grieved the loss of pure pleasure, love's small shadow at our feet. Now I see his final mark—the world without him. Wrens glean seeds beneath the window, and a reckless thrush struts before the door all day.

The world is made of names; my son is learning to speak. He has faith. He believes in things. Rock, I tell him, leaf. No, *this*, he says, holding the rock. *This*, he says, holding up the leaf.

I had never seen her so angry, and her rage revealed a measure of love I had missed. There were many times she might have hurt me that way, and didn't.

My son wakes screaming. His dreams are real; he's riding a horse, and the horse falls down. He's so young, I don't know how to tell him all our joy is wrung from that terror. Did you like it, I ask him. Fall down, he cries, fall down. Did you like riding the horse? And he looks at me, stops sobbing, and says, yes.

I watched a snake crawl onto the lily pads that cover the pond. A fish settled against the leaf, just beneath him. All that afternoon, they never closed their eyes. They barely moved. I still may lose my disaffections and impatience with the world. I may rest.

The sun is a star; what we see, we see by starlight: the clouds, the trees, the cliffs and harsh water. This light is heavenly; it has come to us a long way. It is resting now on a boy's pale arm, and on his small hand that reaches for my shirt.

Beneath the climbing vine, stones rest solidly in themselves. They are so beautiful; they are all I see. How long since I built this wall? I came here for a reason but I forget. There was something that I wanted, I can't remember.

I put asters in a small blue vase. Each morning they open, and they close again each night. Even in this dark room they follow a light which does not reach them. They have bodies. That is all the faith they need.

from Braver Deeds

"Tell brave deeds of war."

Then they recounted tales:
"There were stern stands
and bitter runs for glory."

Ah, I think there were braver deeds.

STEPHEN CRANE

My brother's in Wyoming, and I've had that dream again. We're fishing. The trout rise, take our bait, and keep rising. In love once with a woman, and with my own capacity for pain, I fell in with some cowboys, and broke my neck riding bulls in a little rodeo. That night, drunk in the bunkhouse, not knowing how badly I'd been hurt, I thought it can't get worse than this, but I was wrong. That was twenty years ago. Thunder rolls down South Fork Canyon. The Milky Way is a great river overhead. My brother is in Wyoming. I miss him more than ever when he's there.

My mother was a beautiful woman. She had been a beautiful child. She danced for the soldiers, then, and sang for them, and everyone clapped and cheered. When her period came, she thought she was dying. Her face broke out, and her mother screamed, how could you do this? How will we live? Who will love you now? Years later, my mother turned to me. I was twelve. We'd stopped to rest in a little town. She put her hands on my cheeks. Let me get that, she said, and she dug her nails into me, picking until I bled. That's how it starts, she said, and it wasn't the shock or the pain, it was the look on her face that made me want to cry.

Jupiter, Venus, and Mars are in conjunction beside a crescent moon. Across the road, three young men throw saw blades and knives against a tree. The men shake with a terrible eagerness. Their shrieks are sexual; they could have abandoned themselves to anything, but they've chosen this. That would have killed him, one of them screams. That would have fucking killed him. It echoes off the other side of the canyon, so we must listen to it more than once.

I was home from the hospital and not expected to survive. My mother had come to visit before I died. She needed my attention; she was still weak. She had tried to take her life again. I have trouble breathing, she said, and tapped a gold coin hanging from a choker at her throat. It's to hide the scar, she said, but the coin was too small. I gave her my hand to sit; I gave her my arm to rise. When friends arrived for dinner, she danced for an hour, beautifully. Everyone agreed she had a talent.

Kitty smiled, pressed my hand against the fleshy knot in her belly, and said, it's the child we always wanted, or as close as we'll ever get now. A malignancy, not a pregnancy, was swelling inside her. She'd caress it with her palms, and as the tumor grew, she mothered it; she brought it to term. One night she woke with a fever, and I carried her into the hospital. Her wasted arms and legs made her belly seem even larger than it was. A woman asked, are you in labor? And she said, no. Then the woman asked, but are you expecting? And she said, yes.

I have to look, he said, and peeled away the bandages, unwinding them like a blood-soaked turban. I saw his reflection in the window. His neck was slashed; half his scalp had been sliced away. I wanted to feel sorry for him. I'd seen his leg. Somehow they'd removed the skin, and blood seeped through a layer of gauze and stained the sheets. His face hovered in the dark glass. You have a body, you should love it. That night an old woman lifted my legs from the bed, and set my feet in a little tub of warm water. This might help, she said. Honey, how does that feel? And while I tried to remember the last time I had cried, I cried.

One night, when I was certain she was leaving me, I invented a man I thought my wife might love, and then I tried to be that man. I pulled her to me in the darkness. I kissed her, and she kissed me back. I'm wet, she said. Then she said, what is this? And I felt it too. My nose was bleeding; somehow I'd covered both our faces with blood. This is just like you, she said. You couldn't have planned it better if you'd tried.

Jimmy Rattcliffe played Jesus Christ in a farce at the Little Theatre. He played Santa Claus, the Easter Bunny, and at last, the Savior. Near the back of the hall a man cried out, sinner, Satan, blasphemer, and no one knew if he was part of the play or not. After the show, the man waited for Jimmy, and beat him to death in the parking lot. He and Jimmy had grown up together; they'd known each other all their lives. I had only been home two days, and the world was lost already.

My mother loved violets. When she'd spend whole days in bed for days on end, I'd bring her violets, and put them in a cup on the nightstand by her head. I'd skip lunch all week for the money to buy them, and the florist would nod, and say, violets again. When I'd bring them home, my mother would say, you precious thing. Then she'd look at the flowers and say, they're beautiful, but they never last.

In New Jersey, a couple pulled a man from his car, shot him, and locked him in a box to die. They'd had a plan, but their plan fell through. They were captured, and the woman claimed she'd been forced; she had never wanted to do it. When she testified against her husband, someone shouted, what do you think of your wife now? And he turned, and said, I love her. The stories I must tell myself about myself seem even more pitiful repeated in the history of others.

There was dead space behind an upstairs wall where I knew it was safe to hide. I kept a pillow there and a blanket, and I lit the hiding place with candles. Once, I thought I'd left a candle burning there, but when I looked, everything was fine. An hour later, I looked again. I looked every day, and at last, when I only went to look for fire, I emptied the place of candles. That night I heard voices in the other room, angry shouts, breaking glass, and knew I'd left a candle burning, there was no safe place, and I ran from my bed to check again.

In the final weeks, Kitty was in such pain that to move at all was agony; I couldn't even sit on her bed. It was a relief when she died, to hold her, and rock her in my arms, and know I couldn't hurt her anymore. Later, a friend asked, was it like making love to her? And I suppose it was, but in my grief, it hadn't even crossed my mind.

The burning house turned our nightclothes yellow. Standing at the curb, my brother batted ashes with his hand. We had a puppy, and my mother shouted, where's the dog, and then, my God, where's Cathy? I remember the sound of breaking glass, and walls too hot to touch. I remember pulling my sister from her bed, and leading her out into the world again. I did not wonder, then, how I'd found her, or how my mother could have turned so easily to send me back into the smoke and flames. It was my house; I knew where I was. I could find my way even in the dark.

I was ten, and good at school. Reading meant the newspaper, Cuba, and missiles. I saw circles on a map; all of us inside them would be killed. At the market, my mother fought a woman for a box of powdered milk. My father said, at least we'll go together. I wondered why he went to work, and why I had to go to school. And why was I the only one who stayed awake and planned escape, in a tunnel, underwater, in a car driving somewhere out of range?

My mother cut her toenails and her cuticles every night until they bled. She'd take a little pick and peel away the skin; she'd cut the pale flesh away with shears. I couldn't stop her, and if I asked, are you finished, she always said, no. I sat on her bed and watched; my attention was all I had to give. It was all she ever wanted.

I've been up all night, thinking about a boy I once knew. I can see his body carried along in the dark, and the beach where his body washed ashore. When I fall asleep, it's only for a minute, and when I wake, I want to tell my wife I've had a dream. I dreamed about a wave, I whisper, but she turns away, feigning sleep. I know she's thinking about yesterday, and how the money's gone. She's thinking about yesterday when I threw my glasses at the wall. She's still thinking about yesterday, and the smell of wet plaster, and the bright room with a high ceiling where they fitted a brace to our little boy's right leg.

My father would say, you need a memory lesson, and he'd beat us, first me, then my brother. And I do remember, the little scratches on the banister in the upstairs room, the copper lamps and the flame-shaped bulbs, dark knots on the varnished wall; bamboo curtains creaking as the wind pushed through, the taste of salt, and my brother, shaking as he waited his turn. I took my comfort there; I knew where I was, and what was coming. My father once broke his belt against the back of my legs, and when he saw the welts and the drizzle of blood, he began to cry. I was so frightened to see him change like that, not shouting anymore, but on his knees, sobbing, look what I've done.

I discovered a journal in the children's ward, and read, I'm a mother, my little boy has cancer. Further on, a girl has written, this is my nineteenth operation. She says, sometimes it's easier to write than to talk, and I'm so afraid. She's left me a page in the book. My son is sleeping in the room next door. This afternoon, I held my whole weight to his body while a doctor drove needles deep into his leg. My son screamed, Daddy, they're hurting me, don't let them hurt me, make them stop. I want to write, how brave you are, but I need a little courage of my own, so I write, forgive me, I know I let them hurt you, please don't worry. If I have to, I can do it again.

My mother wouldn't ride, but when the horses had been turned out to pasture, she'd pour salt on our cabin floor, and dance all night for the cowboys. One summer she missed a turn driving into town, and rolled her car into a ditch. She was so happy to be hurt, to be an event. In the hospital she introduced me to a girl who'd spent two days pulling slivers of glass from her teased and bloody hair. My mother asked, did you miss me? But before I could answer, she turned to the girl and said, we have had such a time.

Crushed by love, and by a war that wouldn't end, I abandoned God in nineteen sixty-eight. I thought God had abandoned us all. The world might still exist, if I could hold it in my mind, but there were people, all around me, whose lives were more desperate, and more wonderful, than anything I could imagine. There is an emptiness so great, not even the suffering of others can fill it. God is the chance that anything can happen, then it happens.

Still bandaged, and barely on my feet, I drove into the woods, to a little bar called the Boots and Saddle. I ordered a beer, and the bartender said, this one's on me. A woman in the corner looked up, and whispered, you've been hurt. Then she said, no, you're sick. My baby has been sick like you, she said. She said, you made my baby sick. She shouted, you want to kill my baby, kill my baby, and for a moment, I felt I was flying.

My mother entertained the troops in Vietnam. When she came back, she handed me the photograph of a soldier, and said, he was killed sneaking into camp the night I sang. You may not believe this, she said, but I've never felt as safe as I did while I was there. The Vietnamese soldier in the photograph is hanging by his wrists. A curtain of blood fans out from his neck. His hands are swollen; he was still alive when they strung him up with wire. My mother said, those boys couldn't do enough for me; they treated me like a queen in Vietnam. I still have a picture of the one who gave her his life.

The doctor says, I don't like this, shakes his head, and leaves. I can hear him in the next room. He's found something in the X-ray, and when he comes back he waits for me to ask, what's wrong? Outside, the warm air buoys a perfume of roses, asphalt and ether. Is this the world I just left? Under the knife a dozen times, I always come back stunned by what I've missed: that date palm obscured by the branches of a cedar, the letters on a handmade sign; a child's cough, my fears, how much I love this life.

My mother had the flesh burned from her lips; she had the skin peeled from her face. She wanted to look young again. When the scabs fell away, and she couldn't bear the bright, new scars, she poisoned herself. I have so much to tell you, she said later. She said, I left my body. I knew I was dying, and I could see my body there. I floated away from it, down the hall, and through the door into the street. There were people everywhere, she said. It was beautiful. They wanted me to lead a parade. Mother, stop, I said, I was there.

I want to love you while I can, she said, what's wrong with that? And because I had no answer I looked away, and when I turned to leave, lost consciousness and fell. My arms spun over my head, and my body floated there in the dark. I could feel my heart beating slowly, then slower still, until I felt nothing at all. It was quiet, I was happy, I knew I was dying. I heard a voice call to me from far away. I tried to ignore it, but someone was shouting my name and sounded so frightened, so beautiful and insistent, I had to come back.

Kitty and I were born on the same day. That was a coincidence; there are only so many days. When doctors said I wouldn't live another year, Kitty prayed it could be her instead. Six months later, when she was dying, Kitty thought her prayers had been answered. She didn't believe in coincidence. She was happy the night she died. She said, I did this for you; all these years are for you. She died on my mother's birthday, October fourth, the day of Saint Francis, who once said, praised be my Lord for our sister the death of the body.

The bodies of men and women sometimes ignite from within, and burn from the inside out. Nothing remains but a pile of ash where only minutes before a girl had been lying on the beach, or a young man had complained of the heat and then burst into flame. How can we explain the world? My heart is beating, I can feel it. God loves us more than we can stand.

Last week, a minister and his small congregation paddled boats onto a lake, and tried, like Jesus, to walk on water. They'd intended to test their faith, but instead, tested God, and they drowned. Faith was tested in those who stayed behind and watched from shore. They knew, if one of them, only one, had been able to run across the water, the others might all have been saved.

To survive his years in solitary confinement, a man invented a castle, and filled it with candles, tapestries, silver and wrought iron. Another man imagined a resort, and spent his days setting tables, fixing menus, making beds. All those years, dreaming of the same house, discovering, every night, another room, a hidden passage, a secret chamber, I never thought of the passing days. I fingered the dark molding along the unexpected corridors, hung curtains or set rafters, until the blows of a hammer, or the blood pounding in my ears, would wake me.

My mother practiced yoga. She leaned forward from her waist, pulled her legs behind her neck, and said, my vagina's collapsed; the doctors say there's nothing they can do. In the mental ward she met a young man from Texas. He had small, hard muscles, and his face twitched when he showed me his tattoos. He and my mother talked about home, and madness, about the future and electric shock. They fell in love. When they were released, he terrorized my mother, broke into her house and beat her again and again. I should have had him arrested and put away, but she was so happy, so excited, that I didn't have the heart.

My brother was playing in the car when he slipped, pulled the handle, and cut his thumb off in the door. My father heard the scream, and ran naked from the house. My bike was on the porch, and without breaking stride my father picked it up and tossed it aside. I remember it hovered in the air. I remember my father flying, too. He took off from the porch and sailed above the shrubs, the grass, the newly staked trees, and at last came to rest by the car, where he knelt, and pressed my brother's bloody hand into his chest.

A girl I knew was murdered, and her mother, out of grief, wore the dead child's clothes. Soon she believed she was her own lost daughter. Later, they discovered someone had filmed the girl being killed. How can we bear witness to this? A child dies, and a woman goes mad. A man pays to see the child tortured, and while he watches, comes in his hand. And I tell a story, about a girl I knew, because grief is an echo that calls me, and it's wrong, but it's all I can do.

I saw the carcass of a deer, and turned, and walked toward it. I shuddered at the smell, but went on. I was a boy, my life was still new to me; what could I expect if I should lose it? I leaned toward the body. The deer was moving; bees had made a hive in the open belly. A lulling hum droned from the ribs. Where I thought I'd find blood, and bone, and the pearly organs, there was honey, there was gold.

They bussed us to the induction center. Inside, I spilled a hundred cups of urine and passed out cigars. When they asked, I was deaf, blind. I was nineteen, and I didn't know what else to do. They gave me an intelligence test, and I answered every question wrong. An officer said, we'll give you another test, and each time they did, my intelligence failed. I was alone in a room with two men. They stood beside me with their guns drawn, and gave me one test after another for hours. One of them said, you son-of-a-bitch, the men you came with are waiting for you outside, and we'll keep them there all night if we have to. He didn't understand, I'd have kept them there forever if I could.

When I was five, I knew God had made the world and everything in it. I knew God loved me, and I knew the dead were in heaven with God always. I had a sweater. I draped it on a fence, and when I turned to pick it up a minute later, it was gone. That was the first time I had lost anything I really loved. I walked in circles, too frightened to cry, searching for it until dark. I knew my sweater was not in heaven, but if it could disappear, just vanish without reason, then I could disappear, and God might lose me, no matter how good I was, no matter how much I was loved. The buttons on my sweater were translucent, a shimmering, pale opalescence. It was yellow.

It's Sunday, October ninth, and the earth here is barren after harvest. A cottonwood and a stand of poplars are all that disturb the horizon. A dust devil skips across the stubbled field, and a hawk drifts in and out of the twisting wind. There isn't a single cloud over the valley. The sun is at my back. A crescent moon slips through haze at the lip of the coastal range. I could die today with only two regrets.

Alone in a strange town, sleeping in a strange bed, I woke to thunder, and to hail raking a metal roof. The lightning was so brilliant, I could look away, close my eyes, and still see it in the room. The repertoire of solitude is huge. Last night I spoke to the dead. I called to my wife, come quickly, it's Michael, Kitty, they want to talk. Hurry, I pleaded, it's Mark, it's Ernesto, but it was already too late. I was waking when I cried out, it's my mother.

from If He Had

After the banality of the abyss, what miracles in being!

E. M. CIORAN

I am not an incidental thought of God's. Last night I had a dream. My wife and I were making love when I turned, and discovered our son had hanged himself from a beam in a corner of the room. I woke with my arms stretched out to lift the boy's limp body from the rafters; I could still feel the weight of his body in my arms. I am not an incidental thought of God's. I offer God what happens in time.

Six birds rise in unison from the roof across the street. They circle overhead, then they land again on the building's brick façade. It's dusk, and the birds are a perfect silhouette against the failing light. The dark is almost upon us. There is a ragged pink cloud in the sky; it wasn't there a minute ago. The worst thing you can imagine is not the worst thing that can happen to you.

She called the police the night Peter disappeared, and the police said, there's been a murder, describe your friend. She began to speak, and she could see his body laid out before her. She recalled his eyes, his hair, then his hands, his chest, his teeth. She mouthed every birthmark, every scar; she mothered him with her voice, and fleshed him out with words. When she had finished, she bowed her head as if to kiss him, and whispered a verse she'd memorized as a child. Set me as a seal upon thine heart, as a seal upon thine arm: for love is strong as death.

A woman leans against a tall white pine, looks up into the tree, then lowers her head and stares at the horizon. Her son has climbed into the branches high above her. She's called him down twice, but afraid now her voice might distract him, she stands there silently and waits for him to fall. She knows if he does, there is nothing she can do. A cold wind moves through the tree. She can feel her body stiffen, but does not look up when the child cries out, I can see almost forever.

When your children ask, will you always love me, say you will love them forever, and then tell them what forever means. You can explain the heavens if they ask, and tell them, your bodies are made from the dust of shattered stars. But when they ask you, will I ever die, then lie to them. They're still young, and it might frighten them if you said, no.

There are tracks in the snow outside my window, a tangle of prints in the center of a white expanse. A bird must have landed there, walked in circles and then flown off. The branches of the pin oak are glazed with ice. The moon is rising, and a ribbon of cloud spins slowly over the hills. You can die of happiness, I've seen it. I could die tonight, and be carried away.

Tom Bone fell from deck, and watched as the ship sailed on without him. He tried, at first, to convince himself he wasn't there, then he swam all night. He drifted with a current, and in the morning saw an island, and swam to it, and was saved. There'd been a moment, before dawn, when he'd lost all hope and lowered his head into the water. He was about to take a breath, when he heard a voice say, you're going to live, don't give up, you're going to make it. I have listened to that voice all my life.

My son's small voice wakes me from a dream. He's on the coast with his mother, and when I phone them, he says, I was just dreaming of you. I had something to show you, he says, but you know that, you were here.

That afternoon in the garden, the flowers throbbing in sunlight, the air a drone of sobs, I said, we have witnessed an entire life, and we can measure that life, and hold it in our hearts like a jewel. What if I was wrong? I saw the boy later in a dream, walking with a group of children. He was taller than I remember, and laughing, too busy to answer when I called. If he had died, where had he grown so?

To keep him still, they bandaged his eyes while his small life collapsed within him. But we knew, the bandage was meant to hold what light was left inside.

Fog descends over the tidal surge and the shallow lagoons. The marsh grass and the alders at the water's edge fade, then vanish in the mist. The tan oaks and the redwoods are only shadows that waver for a moment then disappear. The world is beyond us. It is held now in a vaporous light, the smoke from a fire burning somewhere in heaven.

They sat with the boy's body. The body was theirs now. It belonged to them. It had belonged to them once before, but that was in a world they had only imagined, one night, when they'd first thought to invent the boy.

Hummingbirds build their nests under the ferns; little cups of lichen, feathers and moss. They cannot walk, but they can hover in the air. They can fly forward and fly back, and when they move into the light, their frail bodies shine with iridescence. Watching them in the garden, my own voice startles me saying, look, there's my heart.

I followed the mazy fracture on the X-ray, and ran a corresponding hand across my head. I could see inside myself: the fractured skull, eyeless sockets, teeth floating in the milky bones. I was just a boy, and believed I could see myself thinking there. I remember lying in bed after the fall, and someone said, you gave us quite a scare; my God, you were crying tears of blood.

The rain has stopped and there's time, between storms, for a walk downtown. Rainbows marble the oil-stained streets, and lights strung in the sycamores hover like a brilliant cloud. It's dusk, and as you turn toward a cafe, you throw your hand out to shield a boy from the passing cars, but the boy isn't there. You order coffee. The cup is warm in your hands, and you can see your breath hanging in the cold air. The lights at the end of the street are brighter now in the growing dark. They seem to swarm and pulse. They're so beautiful, and for a moment, you think, unendurable, but they're not.

The sycamore leaves are slim green flames just rising from the blistered limbs. Last year's leaves still litter the ground at the base of the trees. The wind has blown them into piles, and the children walk out of their way to crush them underfoot. There is something precious in the empty sky. How many times must I be reminded, nothing dies.

I would live forever if I could, but not like this.

Above the creek, a blue jay sits on a thin, dead twig. He lifts himself with a shrug, and when his body drops, the branch breaks away from the tree and falls. The startled bird falls too, and tumbles with the falling limb, until he remembers, he can fly.

In Missouri there are towns named for saints, for trees, for bad water. There is a cave named for the devil, and cities conjugated like verbs. Moody, Climax, Rocky Comfort—the map is a romance. Where am I now? Walking down 8th Street after rain, I saw another life I might have entered, but didn't.

He was drinking in the airport bar, and I asked, are you coming or going? I have been there, he said, and I almost didn't get back. He said, the engines failed, and we seemed to be falling forever; I've never been so afraid. Then he took a sip of his drink, and rolled back his sleeve. He'd printed his name down the length of his arm, and below that he'd written, Honey, I love you. It's strange, he said, what goes through your mind at a time like that. I hope to God this washes off, he said. My wife just loves to worry.

He wheeled a corpse into the narrow furnace, and said, there's something I want to show you. He lit the gas, and the head rose from the table, the arms flew open and the body sat there for a moment in the fire. The flesh peeled away from the bones, and the bones snapped and burned with a fierce blue flame. When the oven had cooled and the door was opened, the ashes and bits of bone threw off a pale, opalescent light. That light, he said, is what I wanted you to see.

An owl drifts slowly through the canyon where three flickers worry a pitted oak for grubs. Jays make a racket in the redwoods. Mourning doves sit motionless in the orchard. Robins gorge themselves on the pyracantha, and a hummingbird hovers just out of reach. Ravens, wrens, thrushes, hawks. I have tried so hard to be content doing nothing. I thought I'd done nothing all day, and then I remembered the birds.

Last summer, I dug thistles from the orchard, cut the swollen heads from their spiny stalks and put them in a paper sack. When the sack was full I threw it on the slash heap to burn. This morning, when the slash and the deadfall limbs were in flames, I watched the sack curl with the heat; it rocked in the fire and seemed to float there over the coals. Then the sack burst into flame and a silky cloud of thistle down rose with the smoke and drifted to every corner of the field.

I was prepared for anything, the unexpected hemorrhage, my wife's belly swelling with blood, my own hands slick with it. And the shouting, women's cries, and the cries of the newly born. Anything can happen, and that afternoon we found ourselves in the same place at the same time. A baby lies curled and sleeping on my chest, another son, my flower.

Our life is one catastrophe after another. Disaster dogs us. I'm the luckiest man alive, and you know what that means. Earthquakes, landslides, falling trees. Wind and rain and rising waters. What the hell, we survive. The coyotes are screaming on the other side of the field; it's a strange music. The stars are out. It's lovely here, and like the world, I marry you every day.

The passion flowers have bloomed at last on the chain link fence behind the bar. Bamboo rustles in the ocean breeze, and a palm tree sways slowly left and right. Inside, everyone's talking; everyone's telling another sad story. A cypress tree, ancient, enormous, towers over the bar, and every Friday night I step outside alone to look at it.

from Pleasure

Pleasure lies in being, not becoming.

THOMAS AQUINAS

It's a joy to be subtracted from the world. Holding my son's naked body against my own, all I feel is what he is. I cannot feel my own skin. I cannot feel myself touching him, but I can recognize his hair, the heft of his body, his warmth, his weight. I cannot measure my own being, my subtle boundaries, but I know my son's arms, the drape of his legs, smooth and warm in a shape I can measure. I have become such a fine thing, the resting-place for a body I can know.

The Vedas tell us that human perfection is achieved only in dreamless sleep; no desire, no fear, no ego, just a state of pure being. I believe that's true, but waking from a dream to rain drumming the windows and the roof, I draw my legs across the warm cotton sheets, bury my head in the pillows and rest this side of sleep; no longing, no anxiety, no harm done.

A tall man in a white apron and a starched white shirt stands at a table folding napkins. There's a bowl of sliced lemons on the counter; I can smell them. Light seems to pour from the walls. My wife turns to me and says, I love you. She's pleased with herself; she found this place. A bouquet of tulips is reflected in a mirror behind the bar, and so are we. There's a song on the radio I've never heard before—you can't kill me because I'm already dead.

I stood on a narrow bridge where the marsh meets the incoming tide, and I saw two birds. The first one called out softly as it turned and drifted on the wind, while the other one, made of light, slid silently over the surface of the bay.

Three women walked toward me on the street, and all of them were lovely, but one was more beautiful than the rest. Her breasts, loose under a gauzy blouse, swayed with every step, and her nipples carved little circles in the air. As she was about to pass me she dropped her keys, and stopped just an arm's length away. Before I could move, she bent over from the waist, and out of modesty, or courtesy, I might have turned away, but I looked.

I couldn't find the mushrooms under the begonias in the garden, then I remembered I had seen them growing there in a dream. The flowering thistle, dewdrops clinging to the spider's web—it wasn't all a dream. That's coffee I smell, not wood smoke; and here's the glass vial where my wife has saved all our children's teeth.

Since dawn, the dove's melancholic repetitions have haunted the air. Melodies from childhood, oh, please not that. Some memories I can feel in my body like a bruise. Mothers walk by with their little ones, and the dove keeps singing. A mockingbird starts up on a branch nearby: it's call and response—the pitiful piping of the dove, and the giddy exuberance of the mocker. Their music is a clairvoyance. Who knew I'd be whistling by now? Who could have guessed I'd be singing such a happy song?

I took my son into the forest. He is a fearless child, but he was frightened by the woods and never left my side. We found chanterelles under the oaks, and carried them home for dinner. Even in the kitchen my son clung to me. We cooked the mushrooms with a handful of garlic in olive oil and butter. I added chicken, seven lemons, seven limes, and a scoop of cinnamon, why not? Steam from the noodles fogged our windows, so the moon that night was vague, mysterious, but available.

When I was a young man and found I had cancer, my friends held a benefit. There was music and dancing, and when the night was over, they gave me a paper bag filled with cash. My wife then was always worried about money, but whenever she panicked, I reached into the sack and handed her a fistful of bills. I'll never be that rich again. Not a moment escaped me. I had everything I needed and nothing to lose. I've never been happier than when I was dying.

A warm current moved up the coast and brought albacore to our cold waters. I bought a whole tuna at the docks, and took the fish back to my home in the mountains. It was winter, but Brad wanted to cook outside, so we stood in the rain smoking cigars under umbrellas held high above the fire. We grilled the fish in a crust of ginger, lemon grass, cayenne and basil, but we left the meat raw inside and drizzled it at the table with lemon juice, wasabi and soy. While we ate, the rain turned to slush, and long before we had finished, the fire beneath the metal grill sputtered, steamed and went out.

The boys have no idea how beautiful they are, and this, of course, makes them lovelier. They jog in loose formation. They stretch and run and never tire. Their uniforms, bloodied where a steel cleat has caught an ankle, or grass-stained and streaked with dirt after a hard slide, cannot camouflage their sadness or their splendor. They are so lonesome in their bodies.

The signature mark of autumn has arrived at last with the rains: orange of pumpkin, orange persimmon, orange lichen on rocks and fallen logs; a copper moon hung low over the orchard; moist, ruddy limbs of the madrone, russet oak leaf, storm-peeled redwood, acorns emptied by squirrels and jays; and mushrooms, orange boletes, Witch's Butter sprouting on rotted oak, the Deadly Galerina, and of course, chanterelles, which we'll eat tonight with pasta, goat cheese, and wine.

My son says, I wish I could be in my body. You are in your body, I tell him. No, he says, I'm in my self. Only my self, he says, and shakes his head. I wish I could be in my body, he says, and he walks away tapping one hand lightly against his thigh.

Stephen sends me clippings from the *Times*. Joe Black, a pitcher for the Dodgers, is dead. The poet Philip Whalen is dead. A Buddhist Lama, dead for 80 years, sits in a full lotus dressed in a golden robe, his radiant skin still pliant. In Montana, a desperate man feeds a boy to his neighbors; in the New Square Fish Market a 20-pound carp shouts apocalyptic warnings in Hebrew. We can't resist, and though we spend our whole lives trying, can never touch all there is.

We'd been talking about the limits of our resolve, and I admitted that sometimes I resent my own life. Of course my resentment always turns to longing, I said, and I'm filled with the wonder of my existence. Then I think about death, how it offends me, and how I love this life so much I could die of it, and my resentment begins again. While we spoke, a hummingbird hovered above the stream; how hard they both worked, moving constantly just to stay in place.

I woke in panic from a terrifying dream. A rose bush in bloom beside the broken pane of a greenhouse window still lingered in my mind, and I remembered that as I was falling asleep you crawled into bed beside me. Your mother said, Daddy isn't well, and you pulled your fingers across my face. I held you there as long as I could, my hand on your back where I could feel your heart, relentless in its cage of bone.

There was a total eclipse of the sun, and the light at the beach turned vaporous. The air chilled quickly, the wind picked up, and in the weakening light a young woman left her friends at the shoreline and walked toward me. She smiled, held a straw hat up to my chest and said, look. Sunlight passed through the tiny spaces in the weave, and I was covered with dozens of tiny suns, all shrinking to slivers against my skin as the moon slid silently above.

She handed me a piece of salmon, ruby-hued and redolent of wood smoke and the sea, moist, silky with oil. I ate the fish slowly, and told her, I've only eaten salmon like this once, years ago on the Skagit River. She said, this salmon was caught on the Skagit. She went on, but I wasn't listening. I was thinking of eagles in the cedars; raw oysters, fennel bread, salmon and white wine; oyster shells in the middens; ice breaking under our boots on the trail to Fishtown.

My son has drawn two circles, two faces on the asphalt in chalk. He's given each face a nose, and their mouths, two wavy lines, are smiling. My son has made two dim marks on one of the faces, and he tells me, this one can't see because his eyes are too small. I say, that's very sad, but my son says, it's all right, because his friend—whose eyes are slashes of color that dance across his face like flames—sees very, very well.

There wasn't flesh enough to resist the syringe, so I'd drive it in as far as I dared and release the morphine. Her body would stiffen, then relax; she'd catch her breath and release a string of sighs as if she were coming. There was something we could do. It wasn't all a horror.

I rose before dawn, and watched a small cloud blush as the sun
began to rise. My wife and my children kept sleeping, and I had
the quiet house to myself. I let the cat in through the front door,
and out again through the back. I read in silence. This once was all
my life, poems and silence, cutting woodblocks and pulling prints
in my studio day after day. I loved it, but not enough to live alone.
No footfalls, no shouts, no one crying out for me in the night;
no, I could never have lived without the others to forgive me.

Every Wednesday, Fidel brings oysters to the market. I like to eat them with salsa, cilantro and lime. I like to run my tongue along the slick lip of the inner shell and suck them into my mouth. I love knowing they're alive. Fidel wants to know, how many? And when I tell him, I'll start with two, he taps his blunt knife against a block of ice, and shucks three.

It's early winter, and the begonias have delivered a second bloom. Scarlet blossoms hang heavily from their brittle stems; peach-hued blossoms as large as my head mingle with yellow ones, orange, apricot and pink. The annual beds are still an embarrassing spectacle of color—cyclamen, azaleas, even a lily has held off its bloom until now. I step down the stone walk toward the house, absorbed in the dazzle of the garden, and the hummingbird that hectored me all summer when I watered, spins just inches before my face. I stumble on the brick walk, and the small bird hovers over me for a long moment, its crimson head chattering, then swings back to its home hidden deep in the ferns.

I left home when I was seventeen. Seventeen years later you and I were married, and today we have been married for seventeen years. It's a queer calculus. For seventeen years I have turned to you in the dark, and teased your nipples with my tongue. I have watched your body swell with children, and I have seen our children slip startled and wide-eyed into the world. There is a locust that rises from the ground only once every seventeen years. When the time comes, bury me deep. It's only love that's held me here this long, and even in the grave I'll still want you in my bones.

The beans soaking in the steel pot had the luster of polished stones. While they simmered, I sautéed onions, garlic, tomatoes and leeks. There was basil at the bottom of the jar, so I added that, and rubbed a stem of thyme between my palms and let it fall. The kitchen was moist and warm, and the windows steamed over as if curtains had been drawn. When the soup was ready, I lifted a spoonful to my mouth, and before I took a sip, closed my eyes the way I do when I'm about to kiss.

Who would volunteer to live any moment more than once? I might. This morning I smelled freesias in the garden and closed my eyes. Suddenly I was young again, and you were still alive.

When I step in from the deck after smoking a cigar, my wife glares at me and says, you stink—but I can't resist. They punctuate the routine drudgery of a day, and not with a comma, but an exclamation point, a smoky ellipsis of desire . . . . *Robusto, torpedo, maduro:* we need a Romance language to talk about cigars. Buckley once handed me a fat Cubano, a *Romeo y Julieta* made in a factory where a worker reads poetry aloud while the others roll. I could taste the difference. A cigar is never just a cigar; it's a wet kiss, a tongue in your mouth, and both of you burning.

The world cannot be contained. This morning I saw a mockingbird catch a butterfly in midair, and with the bright wings fluttering in its beak, it seemed to have burst into blossom.

The poet is barely visible in the tiny hut suspended over the gorge. He's small, but not insignificant: he's the one who held the brush and made this landscape. There are real ravines, green, green as ink.

Jack is telling a joke at the bar. He begins, two guys are out hunting, and when he's finished, everybody laughs. John shows up and Jack repeats the joke, then Rick arrives, and John says, let me tell him. A guy rides into town on a horse, he says. No, wait, it's a beautician, I don't remember, it doesn't matter, it will come to me, he says, and goes on. They told that joke all night, and I laughed out loud each time.

The fragrance welling up from the petals of the iris is more arousing than a woman's scent. This sexual vertigo is sadly charming; I would penetrate those petals if I could.

A woman kneeling at our table began to tell a story. It was my birthday, she said, I was ten, and I rode my new bike through a pasture on a dare. I was almost across when a bull charged from the far side of the field. I climbed a fence just in time, but the bull made a wreck of my bike. She paused, and I could see that her neck was much whiter than her shoulders or her face—I suppose her hair had just been cut. It's strange, she said, the things you never forget.

Exhausted by the day, and late to bed, we were eager for sleep, but grazed each other, carelessly—a single caress, and we were making love with such ferocity that I understood for the first time why they once called this dying. You came again and again, and I fell deeper inside you, past darkness, past time and all the world, then it was morning.

I bought eggplants at the farmer's market, long and slender, the deep purple reserved for nightshade, castor, the garden's poisonous brood. I was admiring the eggplant's waxy skin, its tender flesh, when a farmer thrust a tomato into my hand. I bit into the firm, red fruit, belladonna's passionate cousin, and ate it under his watchful eye. He looked at me and nodded, as if he knew how far I'd go for pleasure.

Every winter, I climb the apple tree to prune the deadwood and the suckers. I cut the dense, brittle limbs that have sloughed their bark, and let them fall. Below me, my son has gathered all the clippings, and stacked them in a pile. Someday I would like to lie down on a bed of apple boughs like that, and leave this earth as sweet, sweet smoke, but not yet.

I took the children to pick berries, and their fingers and their faces were soon stained red with warm, sweet juice. There were mice running ahead of the children in the furrows, and overhead there were hawks, waiting for them.

When my wife arrived, I was waving a wooden spoon above my head, and dancing, wearing nothing but a towel. It was eight o'clock, warm and still light, even under the redwoods. That morning I'd set four large stones—the last stones in the last wall—and later, I finished framing the guesthouse. That afternoon I folded laundry, cleaned the toilets and caught a gopher in the flower bed; the day went on and on. Chicken with wild mushrooms was heating in the oven. Tracy Nelson was on the stereo singing *Every Night of the Week*. The boys sat naked on the couch, and at last, I dished out dinner, still in my towel.

A sparrow preens its wings on a power line overhead, and casts a filmy shadow across this dusty road, a charcoal drawing erased and redrawn each time the sparrow shudders or twists. The world is re-invented endlessly.

The roads were closed, and the power was out for six days after the storm. I tried to work by lantern light, but what's the use? There was plenty of wine, and after two days, the food in the freezer began to thaw, so we cooked it all. We fed the neighbors chicken with garlic, then herbed sausage with wild rice and beans. We ate by candlelight, and every meal tasted better than the one before. We emptied the pantry, but there were potatoes, a pound of mushrooms, and the last of the raspberries floating in the cooler when a friend walked in with a dripping bag, and said, how do you want to cook this lamb?

Elizabeth fed me—pasta with anchovies, lentils with sage—always a different dish. Gene talked: about love nests, the prairie in winter, and how once, as a child, he'd determined he was God. We sat at a table and looked out at a gingko and a locust, and in spring, a crab apple blossomed beneath the upstairs window. There were paintings on every wall, ceramics on every shelf, and flowers—orchids, zinnias, asters. Elizabeth once made a salad with spinach, walnuts, blue cheese and pear. Then she picked a daylily from a bouquet on the counter, chopped it and sprinkled it over the greens. We spent years that way, feasting on the world.

Acrobats vanished behind a veil of thick, blue smoke. Jugglers tossed hatchets and knives, but it was hot, my son was restless, and we wandered out to the deserted midway. My son ran between the empty amusements while a loudspeaker blared, come see the world's smallest horse. I could hear the animal whinny from its stall while the disembodied voice called, come on over, come on in, this is something that you'll never see again. My son pushed his way through a padlocked gate and was too excited to answer when I called him back, or perhaps he couldn't hear me over the tape's continuous loop crying, he's alive, he's alive, he's alive.

At this hour I like to imagine that everyone I love is sleeping. There may be someone walking through a cold house, a mother up to quiet a restless child, drinking a glass of water, or reading in bed, unable to sleep. I know that somewhere the sun is shining, that people are busy at work or struggling, dying, but here, in the dark, I can imagine everyone at peace, in deep slumber, and it pleases me to think of them that way.

The world is at home in my mind. I can spell *Detroit.* I know where my cats are buried in the orchard. I know the quadratic equation, my mother's maiden name and the suicide squeeze. I know all the words to *A Good Woman's Love* and I can hear them in my head at will. Every thought is like a sweet rolled over the tongue. Even my bad ideas are good.

I'd like to reduce everything to one syllable—a groan, a sigh or startled come-cry. I'd like to hold the world in my mouth. I was looking for a single word, and the word was *you.*

New Poems

New Mexico Journal: Rio Vallecitos

How very large
the world is.

WILLIAM BRONK

I am living in a hogan. The roof fans out from the trunk of a single ponderosa pine. It is the center of the world now. It supports the sky; it holds my life. A breeze passes through the room and moves the curtains at the window. The adobe walls are thick and cool to the touch. Clouds cross slowly overhead. I wish I could hold them. There are faces in the clouds, animals, ruins, a map of the mind rearranging itself. My attention shifts to the unchanging blue, the swirling whites, to the accents of gray in the pines below them. Outside it's dry—the rains are late this year—and a cactus under the barbed wire fence is in bloom. That flower won't last a day, but there are other buds nestled among the brittle spines that will blossom in their turn. I don't know what time it is, but the sun is passing slowly overhead, moving, it seems, against the wind, toward the clouds as they appear above the mountains.

At dusk, the whine of insects. Standing in the pasture, swallows spin all around me, gorging themselves on mosquitoes, flies, and gnats. The birds must notice me, but they twirl unconcerned around my head. They land near my feet, then rise again and twist, this way and that, without moving their wings. The valley is in shadow now, but the sky holds light, and the clouds, still building up over the mountains, coast silently on the gentlest wind. It may be they are motionless, and what I really see is the earth spinning beneath them. There is only the slightest rustle in the cottonwoods. The air has cooled, and tomorrow, I am almost sure, the rains will come.

My father has the power to nap whenever he pleases and rise clearheaded and alert; I can never sleep when there's light. This morning I woke at dawn, read for hours, then turned and fell back to sleep. Later, when it was too hot to write or to draw outdoors, I lay down and slept again. In a dream my son called to me, pulled my arm, and laughing, spun me around by the hand. Tired, finally, of this game, he curled next to me and went to sleep. When I woke up, I thought for a moment he was still beside me, huddled against my chest. This solitude erodes one habit, and magnifies another. I sleep in the daytime; I pass easily, eagerly, from one age to the next.

Here in the valley, sunrise first lights the sky overhead, then the granite and pines on the western ridge. When the sun finally lifts above the mesa to the east, light moves quickly across the valley floor. The shadows travel in starts down the western slope, across the sage and bunch grass in the pastures, and up the orange cliffs to the east when the sun at last is high overhead. The light here is blinding, severe, a threat. The horses stand with bowed heads under the cottonwoods to escape it, and my own eyes rest on a small dark spot the shape of a swallow that passes over feldspar, sandstone, the beige adobe wall.

I often get confused about the stories I tell, and can't remember if I've read them, heard them, or made them up. What does it matter? I am a mystery to myself, but no longer young, my life begins to make a certain sense; the facts I've forgotten, the lies I believe, the should-be's and the might-have-beens. It could even be interesting, a pleasure, this story I've become.

They had warned me about snakes, and today, walking to the stream, I stumbled on a rattlesnake, coiled, and ready to strike. My grandmother used to say, there's a snake in every garden; in this garden, the snake is real.

Tonight, before sleep, I went out to look at the sky. Last night I saw the Milky Way spread out like a stain against the dark; falling stars appeared and vanished in an arc behind the mountains. Tonight there was nothing, just a few scattered points of light. I was ready to go inside when I noticed more stars, and as I sat, the sky grew brilliant with them, until at last the light overtook the darkness and I could see colors. We must adjust to the simplest things, the dark, the light.

I caught my first trout when I was seven, and whenever I see a stream I know holds trout, I can bring it back: the bend in North Fork at the old dairy barn; the smell of alfalfa in the fields beyond; the sound and the smell of water over stones; the electricity in my line; a rainbow, like its name, on the side of the fish; and my father, so happy, standing at my side. Here in the valley the stream meanders and pools around boulders and debris left behind by spring floods. A mile south the water drops from one pool to another down a crease of granite where the mountain falls. I walked two miles of it, not fishing, but looking for fish, and seeing them dart from one side of a pool to another. I filled my pocket with grasshoppers, and when I found a pool I knew held fish, I threw one in, and watched the trout rise, and the hopper disappear. I'd never have thought I could be satisfied just knowing I could catch a fish if I wanted to.

Whenever I travel, the birds tell me first I'm in new country. There are no wrens here to wake me like the ones that wake me at home, but a meadowlark calls every morning outside my window. There are swallows so blue they shine iridescently in the light. So many new songs to learn, new colors, new shapes. Even the names are a gift. I can say: meadowlark, robin, bunting, warbler; western tanager, morning dove, gnatcatcher, oriole. I've seen goldfinch from my desk, a gilded flicker, hummingbirds, swallows, and at night, answering my call from the cottonwoods by the stream, an owl, whose song I know, and reminds me of home.

I am a fearful person. I startle easily, and jump at unfamiliar sounds; I always expect the worst. There are cattle in this pasture, cows, calves, a buckskin mare and colt. They move from one side of the stream to the other, and graze under the cottonwoods, in the open fields, and beside the cedar and piñon. They sometimes bump against the wall beside my bed at night, and their bulk is palpable, eerie and profound. They make a noise like the whimper of children when they're hurt. There has been no moon, and the nights here are deep. The solitude and the empty space distort and magnify every sound. A loose piece of barbed wire grates in the wind outside my window; footfalls and shrill cries wake me in the dark. I stay awake, to listen, and to wonder why I'm not afraid.

On a still afternoon, a sudden, ferocious gust of wind. The door blows open, and papers scatter on the floor. I step outside, and for the first time in a week there are no swallows in the air. A robin stands motionless in the field, then looks from one side to the other; looks up, down, and repeats this motion several times before flying away. A hermit thrush springs onto the boulders at the door. For the longest time he stands with his tail to the wind. He makes motions like the robin, from side to side with his head. The down on his neck is blown back in places by the breeze, and I can see how tiny and frail his body is beneath the feathers. The light suddenly dims; I feel a chill, and just as the thrush flies away, the rains begin.

Shadows passed over the mesa, and I saw six eagles sail across the valley. They rode thermals until they were almost out of sight, then dove, and swung back in circles over my head. The air seemed insufficient to their size—one eagle is enough to fill the sky. Two of the birds veered toward another, and when they met, shook their open beaks and tumbled for a moment before swinging back into an easy glide. They made graceful, abrupt turns, and when they did, the sun hit their backs like a mirror and reflected a fierce copper flash. The sky behind them was so severe that spots of white light began to dance in my field of vision. I don't think I could have watched them any longer if they'd stayed, but they drifted off, with no other purpose, it seemed, than to fly.

Two black geldings have joined the buckskin mare and her colt. They have grazed all afternoon in shade by the stream, but now they gallop and prance from one side of the canyon to the other. When they run full speed across the stream, it sounds like church bells muffled by rain. The colt comes up to me and prances and kicks, then the geldings, snorting and shaking their heads, race toward me and skid to a stop. All four of them jump, run, kick and gallop in circles in the pasture where I'm standing. I laugh, and shout, who are you trying to impress? And suddenly I realize, it's me, they're doing this for me.

I have never experienced such a fracturing of the visual and the verbal in myself. I have been writing in a fever, twelve and fourteen hours a day for the past ten days, and the few times I have tried to draw, my hand felt insensible, like a deaf man who wakes with amnesia and can no longer sign. Last night at dusk I went into the pasture to make etchings of the horses. I could feel an imbalance in my head as I tried to stop thinking, and this was manifested in clumsy, self-conscious plates. But the horses, first fearful and threatening, then cautious but indifferent, began to offer me their forms, and the forms flowed through me, and guided the scribe. I could feel a physical shift as I started thinking, not with my head, but with my hands. I was caught up, and forgot what I was doing. When it was finally too dark to see, I went inside and discovered that my two best efforts had been done on the same plate, one upon the other.

I have long thought of the world as a huge begging bowl, and in this small valley, I feel as if the earth itself has become that bowl, and I am living in the middle of it, alone with the gift of my own life.

The Indians gathered, and I went to see them dance. Their songs were like the songs of birds, the dove, the lark, the hawk. There was the cry of an animal being killed in them as well, and the cry of the animal making the kill. I bought a totem from an Indian woman for my son: a medicine bag with feathers, claws, leather and pelts. I thanked her, and as I turned to leave she reached for me and grabbed my arm. She held my gaze, and I saw a pure desire there, but it was more than sexual. I saw my wife in her eyes; I saw my mother. Wait, she said, take this. And she handed me a long stick covered with deerskin, strange markings, and at one end, a tiny skull painted red with black dots, filled with pebbles. The sun was setting over the mesas, and behind me, a purple band of light like a snake on fire slithered over the mountains.

Ten thousand years ago, glaciers covered these mountains and carved the canyons and the alpine meadows. When the ice sheets retreated, the people came. There were a thousand languages, and in each language, how many stories? Each generation carries with it the stories of the past. The older stories are inevitably lost, but there is an echo of them in the new ones that take their place, and so the generations bear this burden, this legacy and this gift. I am writing a book now about my dead, because their stories are all that remain of them. In time, these stories, too, will vanish. But I think the telling may remain, and sometime, in some future, my stories will return like an echo in another's story, and my dead, if only for a moment, will live again.

In the heat of late afternoon, lightning streaks from a nearly cloudless sky to the top of the far mesa. At dusk, the whole south end of the valley blazes as the clouds turn incandescent with some distant strike. There is a constant congress here between the earth and the sky. This afternoon a thunderstorm crossed the valley. One moment the ground was dry, and the next there were torrents running down the hillsides and arroyos. A quarter-mile off I could see a downpour bouncing off the sage and the fine clay soil. I could see the rain approach, and then it hit, drenching me, and moved on. Ten minutes later I was dry. The rain comes from heaven, and we are cleansed by it. Suddenly the meaning of baptism is clear to me: you can begin again, and we are saved every day.

The district archaeologist is also a poet and a classics scholar. We talk about relativity, creativity, and time. I don't believe in God, she says, but I believe in something like God. In her work, she assembles what remains of the dead. There are only pieces left, but these are enough to bring the dead back to life. She tells me about the Greeks, who believed the past was before them, and the future behind, because the past they could see, but the future was hidden, and always out of sight.

The pottery made in the pueblo is not thrown, but hand-built from coils. The pots are fired in a pit, then covered with manure. Carbon penetrates the clay and turns it black. The pots are polished to a fine luster with a slick, smooth stone. A recurring image carved into the pots is a serpent, or dragon: the guardian of the water. This is a dry land—there is endless talk of water—and this sibilant spirit is alive in the speech of those waiting for the rain, and is in the rain when the rain finally comes.

The tribal guard tells me there is a $20 charge to photograph the cliff dwellings, and a $15 fee to sketch the ruins, so I pass. Then he asks what kind of drawing I do, and I open the sketchbook on the seat beside me, and tell him—charcoal. He waves me through, then motions me to stop. He's been in charge of the ruins for twenty-three years, and complains he cannot make clear to visitors how the houses looked before they fell into ruin. If you can draw that, he says, I'll let you draw for free. There is one structure still standing which I use for a model. I sketch the cliffs, and where there are holes in the wall that once supported lodge poles, I draw a house. He tells me the base of the cliff was flat then, and the houses sat three stories high. He watches me work, and I draw more buildings. I add clouds, trees, and ladders between the levels, and he says, yes, yes, that's it; that's how it was. When I finish, I climb into the ruins, and the profound presence of the place is almost overwhelming. Sitting in a cave, I think, this is where they ate, slept, made love. Looking out the entranceway formed by pink volcanic rock, I think, this is what they saw. Two ravens hold themselves in the breeze that swirls through the canyon, and above me, on the smooth surface of the rock where the highest level of the houses would have stood, I see someone once carved the image of a bird.

Coming down the mountain today I passed an old general store, then stopped, turned around and drove down the rutted drive to the front of the building. I had no reason to be there, but the place called to me. The building was cavernous. The plaster walls were cracked, and the high ceilings were stained and dingy. The few dilapidated shelves were nearly empty; some canned foods, laundry soap and soda were about all that was left. The place seemed haunted—it depressed me—but when I turned to leave, I saw what had drawn me there. In a corner, on a shelf just a few feet from the ceiling, was a triumph of the taxidermist's art, a two-headed calf floating serenely over the room, looking both left and right at once.

As if the sky and the high plateaus were not enough, here is a canyon colored like a child's box of crayons. There are strata of purple, scarlet, yellow, and beige. Small buttes that look like wedding cakes rise up out of the gorge, each layer distinct and otherworldly. There is a shade of green in the small hills surrounding these outcrops I have not seen anywhere else: there are traces of sage, olive, turquoise, the sea, but also sulfur, graphite, and blood. A huge portion of the mountain has fallen away from the side of a cliff creating a natural amphitheater. Echoes are amplified and return resonant and strong. I sit and listen to the split-tailed swifts that nest in the cliff. They whistle, and the echo makes them seem larger, and stronger, and nearer than they really are.

I picked sage and cedar, and wrapped them up with strong, thin lengths of grass. The air was heady with the aroma of the crushed herbs. A boy at home has been sick, so I pulled a piece of sage from the smudge stick, lit it in a little shell, and prayed for him as the smoke swirled around to fill the room. There were no clouds visible outside the window, but just as I said, amen, a single clap of thunder struck the house and echoed down the canyon. I don't know if our prayers are ever answered, but I know they're heard.

This morning a pair of flickers bounced and shrieked on a limb of the dead cottonwood outside my window. A little mask of red glistened around the face of the one closest to me. I took my coffee out into the pasture like I've done every morning, and the cows and their calves stood in a cluster at the barbed wire fence and stared at me. An enormous bull stood behind them and held my gaze. One cow walked slowly around the side of the house, caught my eye, then as if embarrassed, turned sideways but still cocked her head to keep me in sight. The four horses walked across the stream and came up to me. First the colt and then its mother bent their heads and nuzzled my arm. I have wanted to touch these horses for weeks. I don't want to believe they know I am leaving; this is just a coincidence, but I'm part of it. This place has been like a world within a world. I am not returning to my life, but to the rest of it.

In the Face of It

The worst thing about death must be the first night.

JUAN RAMÓN JIMÉNEZ

When Elizabeth had died, Gene told me about two stars seen orbiting in tandem. They revolved in perfect symmetry, one around the other, but their locked orbits became unstable, and the stars spun out of control. One star fell into a black hole, and the other was flung deep into space. I know Gene identified with one of the stars, but I couldn't begin to imagine which.

I once found a smooth, round stone, and I carried it in my pocket. If I'd believed in luck, I would have carried it for luck, but all I wanted then was ballast, something dense and durable—the weight of the world. This morning, after a hard rain, a bird is singing in the ferns below the house. Little wren, my stone, I would sail you across the sky.

The skunks and the deer are in rut again. They bolt from the roadside and stagger into traffic, blind with lust. A skunk was hit on the highway north of town. There was a long streak of gore, a greasy smear on the asphalt. Whoever passed it looked away, but they couldn't escape the stench. It's autumn. The monarchs have returned to the eucalyptus grove, persimmons ripen on their slender stems, and the walnut drops its leaves. In the desert, where the war goes on another year, yellow dates hang in heavy clusters from the palm trees.

Shards of pottery blanket the gopher mounds in the orchard: white stoneware, Blue Willow china, broken bits of carnival glass. I've found cup handles, crockery, bear's teeth and oyster shells, an obsidian scraper and the bones from a man's hand. The gophers burrow through the earth as if it was a churning sea, and the dead and the things they cherished do not rest easy.

Driving north along the coast, I glance up Swanton Road where it drops to meet the highway. A truck piled high with cordwood is parked on the shoulder, and on top of the wood, a young woman with long blonde hair sits naked, her weight resting on her arms, her head thrown back, her breasts thrust forward. I fix her in my gaze until my car speeds by and she's gone. That was twenty years ago. This morning I passed that same spot, and looked for her the way I always do, and as always, I thought I saw her for just a moment, and I drove on.

Last night I dreamed about a bobcat, and this morning I found one sleeping beneath the persimmon tree. I was almost close enough to touch him, when he woke, fixed me with his eyes and disappeared into a thicket. The air was damp with last night's rain. The matted leaves cushioned my steps, and persimmons blazed in the branches of the tree like a hundred suns. I don't know if the cat appeared because I dreamed of him, or if I dreamed of him because he was so near.

A raven calls out overhead. He knows what a raven knows, and he sings what every raven sings. He is the forest's darkest thought, and when he flies, he punishes the air with his wings. Once he's passed, I hum a song to myself, one I've never heard before, one I make up as I go. A raven doesn't live forever, but the raven doesn't know.

Fissures in the bedrock open and shift, and each day the house tilts a little more toward the stream. At night, I can hear the granite shelf creak under its own weight, and when I hold my breath, I hear the water percolate beneath us. In the morning I see it running from the spring box, and I gather it in, and drink it.

This tumor is smaller than the last one, he said. I'm going to cut it out, and then do my best to stitch you back together. He leaned forward, and pulled a blade across my leg. Smoke rose from the open wound as he cauterized the tiny veins, and while he worked, he spoke to me. Every body is a machine, he said. When they break, I fix them. But there's an art to it, he said. We have to coax some kind of magic or luck out of the body. Some patients die, he said, and others find a way to beat the odds. That's what I expect of you. Do you know what I'm saying, he asked? I nodded while my breath kept pace with the morphine drip. Good, he said, and he put his knee on the table for a better purchase. I watched my leg jump and fall as he jerked on the sutures. That should hold, he said, but you're going to feel it for a while.

The earth submits to seasonal drift. The stars slide, and the planets swing higher over the horizon every day. This morning the sun sent a shaft of light through a rift in the redwoods; it followed the steep angle of the canyon, skirted the stream, the wild azalea, the granite cut bank, and shone on the brick stoop beneath the stone arch at our gate. It rested there only for a moment, but my son found it. He sat there warming himself, and anyone watching the light play over his body could have believed he was made of gold.

I asked the sitter if there had been any calls, and she told me, just one. She pointed to a name she'd written on a slip of paper—Johnny Walsh—and beside it she'd written the word *mad*. She said, I answered the phone, and a man said, this is Johnny Walsh. When I said, this is Ashley, he started screaming. He said, I'm going to kill you. He said, I'm going to stab you in your eyes. I was scared, she said, so I hung up the phone. When she finished telling me what had happened, I called the sheriff, and when he arrived, he showed us a photograph and said, have you ever seen this man? This is Johnny Walsh. He's been doing crimes in the valley, and we know he's involved with a girl named Ashley. I can see this is just a coincidence, he said, but I had to check it out. In the morning I read the crime report—how she hadn't seen it coming.

My son says, you'll be mad at me, and his mother asks, why? I called Daddy stupid, he says, and his mother wants to know when. I did it all day tomorrow, he says, and I'm so sorry.

In western Massachusetts, a man wandered into the woods to live alone. He tried hunting, but the only animals that stood their ground, the only animals he could catch were skunks. The man was sprayed, of course, but he caught them, ate them, and dressed in a cloak of rancid pelts. When he was found, the scent was on his breath, his skin, and when I heard his story, I thought, comrade.

Sparrows glean the air for gnats, and over the bluff two hawks hold, motionless above the breakers. Wind in the redwoods, a rush in the blood; I can feel the breeze that buoys the birds about to carry me away.

Light has a history. Wheeled out from the cosmos, or unleashed by a sputtering match, light bathes us, caresses our contours. Last night, lying in the dark, a light flared inside my head, and though I tried to find the source, it was much too bright to see.

Damselflies couple in midair, the blue pearls of their bodies iridescent in the sunlight. A dead wren lies in the middle of the path. My brother understands this is not where I want to be. An envelope arrived this morning—he'd filled it with sage.

Near midnight, walking uphill by starlight, the ground still wet, the air brisk and moist after the storm, I was startled by a pocket of warm air. A breath from the mountain, the river, the trees? I turned to look. No, the moon.

Gary Young is a poet and artist whose honors include grants from the National Endowment for the Humanities, the Vogelstein Foundation, the California Arts Council, and two fellowship grants from the National Endowment for the Arts. He has received a Pushcart Prize, and his book of poems *The Dream of a Moral Life* won the James D. Phelan Award. He is the author of several other collections of poetry, including *Hands; Days; Braver Deeds*, which won the Peregrine Smith Poetry Prize; *No Other Life*, winner of the William Carlos Williams Award of the Poetry Society of America; and *Pleasure*. He is the co-editor of *The Geography of Home: California's Poetry of Place* and *Bear Flag Republic: Prose Poems and Poetics from California*. Since 1975 he has designed, illustrated and printed limited edition books and broadsides at his Greenhouse Review Press. His print work is represented in numerous collections, including the Museum of Modern Art, the Victoria and Albert Museum, the Getty Center for the Arts, and special collection libraries throughout the country. In 2009 he received the Shelley Memorial Award from the Poetry Society of America. He teaches creative writing and directs the Cowell Press at the University of California Santa Cruz.